Christina Ricci

Julia Holt

Published in association with The Basic Skills Agency

Hodder & Stoughton

A MEMBER OF THE HODDER HEADLINE GROUP

Acknowledgements
Cover: Stewart Cook/Rex Features

Photos: p 2 © Lucy/All Action; p 5 © Alpha; p 7 © Orion Pictures International/Ronald Grant Archive; p 10 © Orion Pictures Corporation/BFI Films; p 13 © New Line Productions, Inc./Topham Picturepoint; p 18 © Barry Wetcher/Buena Vista/Ronald Grant Archive; p 21 © Reuters NewMedia Inc./Corbis; p 26 © Phil Ramey/All Action

Every effort has been made to trace copyright holders of material reproduced in this book. Any rights not acknowledged will be acknowledged in subsequent printings if notice is given to the publisher.

Orders; please contact Bookpoint Ltd, 39 Milton Park, Abingdon, Oxon OX14 4TD. Telephone (44) 01235 400414, Fax: (44) 01235 400454. Lines are open from 9.00–6.00, Monday to Saturday, with a 24 hour message answering service. Email address: orders@bookpoint.co.uk

British Library Cataloguing in Publication Data
A catalogue record for this title is available from The British Library

ISBN 0 340 80094 1

First published 2001
Impression number   10 9 8 7 6 5 4 3 2 1
Year   2007 2006 2005 2004 2003 2002 2001

Typeset by SX Composing DTP, Rayleigh, Essex
Printed in Great Britain for Hodder & Stoughton Educational, a division of Hodder Headline Plc, 338 Euston Road, London NW1 3BH by Redwood Books, Trowbridge, Wiltshire

Contents

1 Early Years

Christina Ricci
has been an actress
for half her life.
Her family joke
that she's been an actress
all her life!

She is the baby of the family.
As a child
she was always trying
to make her family laugh.
'She lived for making
her brothers and sister laugh,'
says her mum.

Christina Ricci has been acting for a long time.

Christina was born in California
on 12 February, 1980.
Her mum used to be a model.
Her dad is a lawyer.
She has two older brothers
and an older sister.

The family moved house
when Christina was seven.
They moved across the USA
to New Jersey.
All Christina wanted to do
was play football.
Little did she know
what was in store for her.

That year her school put on a play.
It was called 'The 12 Days of Christmas'.
A little boy called Nicky
had a part in the play.

Christina teased Nicky all the time.
One day he hit her hard.
He was thrown out of the play.
Christina got his part.

On the night of the play
all the parents came to watch.
Nicky's mum was a film critic.
She told Christina's mum
to get her an agent.
She thought Christina could get a job on TV,
making adverts.
So that's what they did.

Casper was one of Christina's first films.

2 Getting Started

For the next year
Christina worked on TV adverts.
Her mum approved.
Christina was bored at school.
Making adverts kept her out of trouble.
Working made life interesting.

Christina spent a year making adverts.
Then she landed her first film job.
She played Cher's little girl
in the film *Mermaids*.
She was only nine years old
but she made friends with Cher.
They are still friends today.
Cher says that Christina
was just like her -
but in a little body!

Mermaids was one of Christina's first films.

Winona Ryder was also
in *Mermaids*.
Winona's boyfriend at the time
was Johnny Depp.
He came to the film set
many times.
Johnny was going to be
very important in Christina's life.
Christina just didn't know it yet.

Mermaids was a very good start
to Christina's career.
It was a wacky film
and a big success.
Christina was a natural actress.

3   The Addams Family

In 1991, Christina got her big break.
She played Wednesday Addams
in *The Addams Family*.
The film made her famous.

It was a kooky, spooky film
about a strange family.
In the film, Wednesday
and her brother Pugsley
put arsenic in some lemonade.
They sell it at the school play.
The play is ruined.
The film made $113 million.

The Addams Family was a huge success.

Christina was a clever girl.
She started reading at the age of three.
When she was filming
she had a teacher with her.
In between films
she went home to her family.
She was happy to be home
but after two weeks or so
she was bored.

She was soon back
making the second
Addams Family film.
This time Wednesday and Pugsley
go to a summer camp.
They manage to spoil it
by burning down the camp!

4 Difficult Times

When Christina was 14 years old
her parents split up.
Her mum got custody
of the children.
She got a job as an estate agent.
They had moved to Manhattan.

Christina lost touch
with her dad.
She stopped eating
and started jogging.
She got very thin.

At the time she was making the film
Now and Then with Demi Moore.
Christina wanted to be thin
like Demi.
It made her very sick
for a time.

Christina starred with Demi Moore (second from left) in
Now and Then.

For the next two years
Christina was never alone
when she made a film.
Her mum always came with her.
They travelled
as far as Ireland together.

They became very close.
Christina says
that as she grows up
she gets more like her mum.
'You always become
like your parents.
You just can't avoid it.'

Christina was always cast
as a mixed-up teenager.
In *Casper* she played
the little ghost's friend
and side-kick.
She was also in the Disney film
That Darn Cat.

By the time she was 17
Christina was type cast
as a children's film actress.
Everywhere she went
people called her Wednesday.
She was fed up with it and said:
'I never want to be in
one of those films again.'

Christina's films were successful
but she wanted to grow up.
She didn't want to be
a child star for ever.
She didn't want to be burnt out.
That had happened to too many others.
Christina was asked
to make a third *Addams Family* film.
She turned it down.

Then, in 1997,
The Ice Storm
changed her life.

5 All Grown Up

In *The Ice Storm*
Christina plays a girl
whose family is breaking up.
In the film she has to go to bed with a boy.
Both their parents
had to be there for the filming.
It was very difficult
for both of them.
She said,
'We were both kind of nervous.'

The Ice Storm
was a very successful film.
Christina learnt a lot
from the other stars in the film.
She says, 'I grew up . . . finally.'

Christina learnt a lot from her co-stars in *The Ice Storm*.

Next Christina starred
in three films with Johnny Depp.
She had first met Johnny
when she was nine years old.

The first film was
Fear and Loathing in Las Vegas.
It is a film about a writer
who takes a lot of drugs.
It was a difficult film to make.
Christina only had
a small part –
but she was very happy
to work with Johnny.

Their next film together
was a big success.
It was called *Sleepy Hollow*.
It is a horror film
based on a very old story.
It was filmed in England.

Johnny plays a policeman
called Ichabod Crane.
He goes to Sleepy Hollow
to solve some murders.
Headless bodies have been found
in a scary forest.
The locals say
the headless horseman did it.
But Ichabod doesn't think so.

He goes into the scary forest
with his love, Katrina.
Christina plays the role of Katrina.
They solve the murders.
It is a magical film
full of fairy story people and animals.

Johnny and Christina are good friends.

Then in 2000
Christina and Johnny
made their third film together.
It is a film called
The Man Who Cried.
It is set in World War II.
Christina plays a refugee.
She runs away from Germany
to Paris.
She meets a gypsy
played by Johnny.

6   The Present Day

Christina likes making films
because she gets to travel.
She often flies across the USA
to try out for films.

She likes the East coast best.
It often snows there.
She also likes watching
the trees change colour.

These days she lives
on the West Coast in Hollywood.
She lives there
with her boyfriend Matthew
and her two cats
Virgil and Vert.

Christina has managed
to grow up in the film world.
She has done this she says,
'by not getting too wrapped up in it.'

She was a child star
and now she is a grown-up star.
She has her own
production company.
She calls it Muse Production.
Now she is writing
her own film scripts.

Christina has three films
in the pipeline at the moment.
They are all very different.

One is a thriller
with Kim Basinger
called *Bless The Child*.

The second is called
Prozac Nation.
It is about a depressed writer.

In the third, Christina
is down to play
a Russian kick boxer
in the film *Andrenalin*.

Christina is going to be a huge star.

Christina is now playing parts
where she can show
her acting talents.
Her career as a grown-up actress
is only just starting.
And it looks like
she will be
a very big star.